weblinks

You don't need a computer to use this book. But, for readers who do have access to the Internet, the book provides links to recommended websites which offer additional information and resources on the subject.

You will find weblinks boxes like this on some pages of the book.

weblinks

For more information about a specific topic here, go to www.waylinks.co.uk/series/religiontoday/Buddhism

waylinks.co.uk

To help you find the recommended websites easily and quickly, weblinks are provided on our own website, **waylinks.co.uk.** These take you straight to the relevant websites and save you typing in the Internet address yourself.

Internet safety

↗ Never give out personal details, which include: your name, address, school, telephone number, email address, password and mobile number.

↗ Do not respond to messages which make you feel uncomfortable – tell an adult.

↗ Do not arrange to meet in person someone you have met on the Internet.

↗ Never send your picture or anything else to an online friend without a parent's or teacher's permission.

↗ If you see anything that worries you, tell an adult.

A note to adults
Internet use by children should be supervised. We recommend that you install filtering software which blocks unsuitable material.

Website content

The weblinks for this book are checked and updated regularly. However, because of the nature of the Internet, the content of a website may change at any time, or a website may close down without notice. While the Publishers regret any inconvenience this may cause readers, they cannot be responsible for the content of any website other than their own.

WAYLAND

Buddhism

Kathryn Walker

WAYLAND

First published in 2007
by Wayland

Copyright © Wayland 2007
This book is based on *21st Century Buddhism* by Anita Ganeri
originally published by Wayland.

Wayland
338 Euston Road
London NW1 3BH

Wayland Australia
Level 17/207 Kent Street
Sydney, NSW 2000

Produced for Wayland by Discovery Books
Consultant: The Clear Vision Trust (www.clear-vision.org)
Maps and artwork: Peter Bull

British Library Cataloguing Publication Data

Walker, Kathryn
   Buddhism. - (World religions today)
   1. Buddhism - Juvenile literature
   I. Title
   294.3

ISBN 978 0 7502 5267 6
Printed in China

Wayland is a division of Hachette Children's Books,
an Hachette Livre UK company

The publisher would like to thank the following for permission to reproduce their
pictures: Corbis/Hugh Sitton/ Zefa cover, Bridgeman Art Library
www.bridgeman.co.uk/ Ashmolean Museum/University of Oxford 6, National
Museum of India, New Delhi, India 18, 24; CIRCA Photo Library/William Holtby
16, 22, 44; Clear Vision Trust 43; Corbis/Keren Su 29; Exile Images/N. Cooper 25,
H. Davies 40; Robert Harding Picture Library 4, J. Sweeney 10, A. Woolfitt 13, D.
Traverso 15, G. Hellier 28, D. Beatty 34, A. Woolfitt 35, U. Gahwiler 37;
Hutchison Picture Library 7, 19, 20, 33, 41; Ann and Bury Peerless 8, 9, 11, 17, 38,
39; Topfoto 21, 31, 36, 42, 45; ZUL 23, 27, 30, 32

Contents

Note

There are often two spellings for the key terms in Buddhism, depending on whether they are written in Pali or Sanskrit, two ancient languages of India. For example, the Pali word for the Buddha's teaching is Dhamma; the Sanskrit is Dharma. (Throughout this book, the most commonly known spelling is used.)

Introduction

Buddhism is one of the world's main religions. It began about 2,500 years ago when an Indian prince taught people how to be free of suffering. His name was Siddhattha Gotama, but he became known as the Buddha. This means the 'Enlightened one' or 'One who knows the Truth'. Buddhists use his teachings as a guide for living and understanding life.

The Buddhist world

During the Buddha's lifetime, thousands of people in India became his followers. Many gave up their homes and travelled about, spreading his teaching.

Buddhism spread through Asia and it mixed with local beliefs in each country. Today there are about 400 million Buddhists. In some countries, the population is mostly Buddhist. These include Thailand, Cambodia, Myanmar, Bhutan and Sri Lanka.

The Buddha's teaching

Buddhism is an unusual religion because it is not about believing in

➤ *This monk in Sri Lanka is honouring the Buddha by bowing and making offerings to a statue of him.*

a God. The Buddha was not a God, but a human being who knew the truth about life. Understanding this truth is known as **Enlightenment**. Through the Buddha's teaching, others can also become Enlightened.

Modern changes

Over the last two hundred years, the popularity of Buddhism has decreased in some countries. This is partly because people have become more interested in wealth and possessions. Also, in some countries Buddhists have been punished for their beliefs.

At the same time, Buddhism is becoming more popular in Europe, North America and Australia. Some Buddhist practices, such as **meditation** (see page 9) are now a part of many people's everyday lives.

▼ *This map shows the number of Buddhists in the world today. Remember when you read the map that some countries, such as Tibet, have small populations but their religion is still mainly Buddhism.*

weblinks

For general information about many different aspects of Buddhism, go to
www.waylinks.co.uk/series/religiontoday/Buddhism

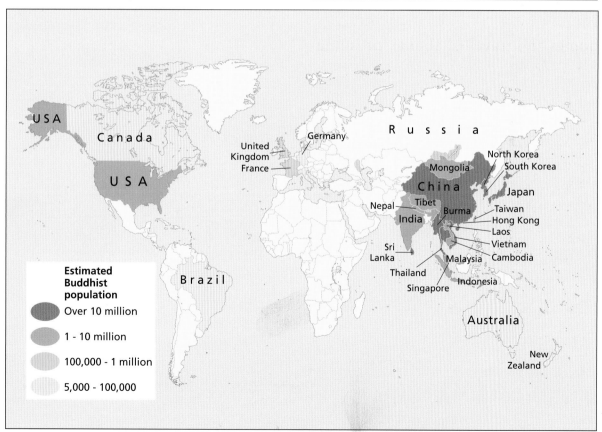

Estimated Buddhist population

- Over 10 million
- 1 - 10 million
- 100,000 - 1 million
- 5,000 - 100,000

1 History of Buddhism

Siddhattha Gotama was born in about 563 BCE in Lumbini, now in the country of Nepal. What we know about Siddhattha comes from the ancient Buddhist writings. There are also many legends about his life. However, these were written centuries after his death and may not be accurate.

Birth of the Buddha

Legend says that Siddhattha was the son of an Indian king. His father was King Suddodhana. His mother, Queen Maya, died seven days after his birth. He grew up in a royal palace.

A wise man called Asita foretold Siddhattha's future. Asita told the king that his son would either be a great ruler or a great teacher. He said that if Siddhattha ever stopped to think about suffering, he would become a teacher.

The king wanted his son to become a great ruler, so he kept Siddhattha away from suffering. Siddhattha

▼ *This carving shows the birth of the Buddha. It dates from the 2nd or 3rd centuries CE.*

lived safely in the palace and did not see the outside world. When he was 16 years old, he married a princess from a nearby kingdom.

➤ *This tree is in the garden in Lumbini, Nepal. It is where people believe the Buddha was born. Buddhist prayers are written on the flags.*

Religion in India

Siddhattha was born at a time when religion was changing in India. People were questioning old ideas.

People in India belonged to different groups or **castes**. The type of work that people did and their wealth depended on which caste they were born into.

Siddhattha taught that the caste that people were born into was not important. What really mattered was how people behaved. He said that the path to Enlightenment (understanding the truth) was open to everyone. It didn't matter whether they were rich or poor.

The Four Sights

Siddhattha lived very comfortably in his father's palace. But his life changed when he was 29 years old.

Siddhattha disobeyed his father's orders and went for a ride outside the palace walls. On his ride he saw a hunched old man, a sick man and a dead body. He was horrified to discover that pain and suffering was part of normal life.

Then Siddhattha saw a holy man. This man had given up his home and belongings to search for true happiness. He owned nothing, but he looked very contented.

That night, Siddhattha decided to leave his royal life. Secretly, he said goodbye to his wife and baby son.

▼ *This is part of a painting showing the Four Sights that Siddhattha saw on his ride. The last of them was the holy man, shown on the right.*

He cut off his hair and put on a simple robe. Then he began life as a wandering holy man with no money.

Enlightenment

Two religious teachers taught Siddhattha how to meditate. Meditation is a way of calming the mind. It helps people to understand the way things are in life.

Next, Siddhattha spent six years in the forest with five holy men. He lived a hard life that he thought would make him wiser. But he still did not find truth.

Siddhattha sat under a tree to meditate. After many hours, he understood the way out of suffering. He was Enlightened. Ever since, the tree has been known as the **Bodhi Tree,** or Tree of Enlightenment.

➤ This image is from a temple in Vietnam. It shows Siddhattha meditating under the Bodhi Tree. There are many statues like this one. They remind people of the story of the Buddha's Enlightenment.

The first teaching

The Buddha continued meditating until he was filled with peace and happiness. He then decided to teach others what he knew.

The Buddha found the five holy men who had been his companions in the forest. He gave his first teaching to them. His words were so powerful that the holy men quickly gained Enlightenment.

Travelling and teaching

For the next forty-five years, the Buddha travelled around northeast India teaching people. His followers became known as the **Sangha**. The Buddha helped many people to reach

▼ *This is the Dhamekh Stupa in Sarnath, India. It is said to stand on the spot where the Buddha gave his first teaching after his Enlightenment.*

Enlightenment. They were known as **arahants** and also became teachers.

In the year after his Enlightenment, the Buddha visited his family. His father became an arahant and his young son became a monk.

Passing away

At the age of about 80, the Buddha became ill and knew his life was ending. He set out with his monks on a final journey. Outside the village of Kushinagar, the Buddha lay down in

▲ *This statue in Sri Lanka shows the Buddha's parinirvana. Legend says that the Buddha lay on his right-hand side when he died and that an earthquake shook the earth.*

a grove of trees. He reminded the monks that everything changes and passes away. Then he died. This event is known as the **parinirvana**.

The Buddha's body was cremated (burned). His ashes were divided into eight parts and given to eight different rulers. Special buildings called **stupas** were built over them.

Buddhism splits

The Buddha's teachings were not written down in his lifetime. Instead, his followers memorized them and told them to others. Nothing was written down until several centuries after the Buddha's death.

Soon, different groups of monks began to disagree about what the Buddha had taught. The main disagreement was about how monks and nuns should live. Between fifty and a hundred years after the Buddha's death, Buddhism split into two groups. These are known as **Theravada** and **Mahayana**. You can read more about them on page 18.

Buddhism spreads

Buddhism spread quickly throughout India and the rest of Asia (see map).

▼ This map shows how the two main types of Buddhism spread out of India.

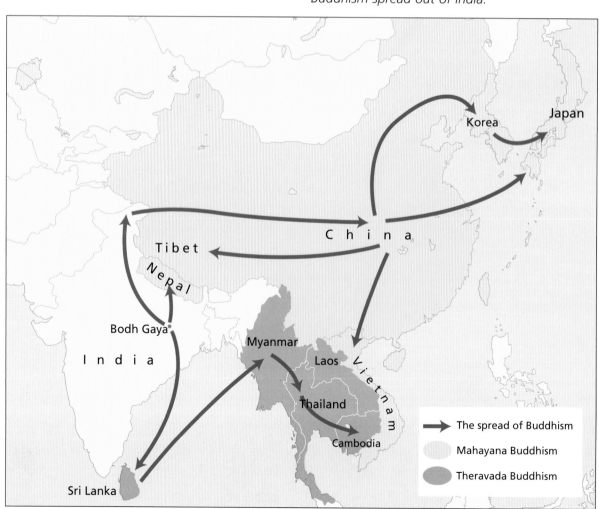

Korea

Japan

C h i n a

Tibet

Nepal

Bodh Gaya

Myanmar

Laos

Vietnam

India

Thailand

Cambodia

Sri Lanka

→ The spread of Buddhism

Mahayana Buddhism

Theravada Buddhism

Buddhism reached China in the 1st century CE. But by the 12th century CE, Buddhism had almost disappeared from its home in India. There are two possible reasons for this. One is that it became part of local religions. The other is that because Buddhism is a peaceful religion, it was easier for people of other religions to invade India. Many Buddhists died.

Emperor Ashoka

The rule of the great Indian emperor (ruler), Ashoka Maurya, began in 273BCE. He took control of most of India through a series of wars.

In one battle, 100,000 people were killed. Ashoka felt horror and guilt for the suffering he had caused. After that, he became a Buddhist. His rule was based on respect for all living things.

Throughout his empire, Ashoka built pillars on which orders were carved. These told people to live honest and generous lives. He also sent people to other countries to spread the Buddha's teachings.

► *The famous lion capital (top) from Ashoka's pillar in Sarnath, India. The four back-to-back lions were Ashoka's symbols. They are now the symbol of India.*

2 Beliefs and sacred texts

Different groups of Buddhists practise their religion in different ways. But they all share the same basic beliefs. For example, Buddhists believe that after dying we live many more lives.

The Buddha's teachings are called the **Dhamma**. They are written down and explained in the Buddhist **sacred** (holy) texts, or writings. Unlike many other religions, Buddhism does not have just one sacred book. Each group of Buddhists has its own set of writings.

The turning of the wheel

In his first teaching, Buddha said that life was like a wheel. Everyone was turning in a cycle of birth, death and rebirth. This wheel is kept turning by **karma**. Karma is people's actions and the effect they have.

The only way to escape the cycle of death and rebirth, is to move towards **nirvana** or Enlightenment. This is a state of perfect wisdom and kindness. Kind and wise behaviour brings you closer to Enlightenment. Selfishness and unkindness leads you away from it.

Three Marks of Being

The Buddha also taught that all things in life are marked in three ways. These are:

1 Suffering. This includes pain and illness. It can also be boredom or dissatisfaction.

2 Change. Everything always changes and nothing lasts forever.

3 No fixed self. Everything about us changes, including our thoughts and feelings. Therefore nothing about us is fixed, not even our own self.

The five parts of a person

The Buddha taught that humans are made up of five parts. These are: the body, feelings, senses, thoughts and awareness.

▼ This painting from Tibet shows Yama, the Lord of Death. He is holding the Wheel of Life. It represents the cycle of birth, death and rebirth. Around the outside of the wheel are the different stages of a person's life. Inside are some ways in which a person might be reborn.

The Four Noble Truths

The Buddha explained why people feel dissatisfied and how they can find happiness. This teaching is called the Four Noble Truths.

1 Everyone experiences suffering

2 Suffering is caused by greed

3 There is a way to end suffering

4 The way to end suffering is to follow the Noble Eightfold Path

The Noble Eightfold Path

The Buddha taught eight ways in which people should live. This is called the Noble Eightfold Path.

1 Right understanding – seeing that the Buddha's teaching is true

2 Right intention – thinking about people in a kind way

3 Right speech – not telling lies or speaking harshly

4 Right action – treating other living things well

5 Right livelihood – doing a job that helps the world and does not harm people or animals

▼ *These images are from a temple in Myanmar. They show the Buddha teaching the Four Noble Truths to the five holy men.*

6 Right effort – doing our best to be kind and not do harm

7 Right state of mind – being aware of what you are doing, feeling and thinking

8 Right concentration – using meditation to calm your mind

Nirvana

Nirvana is the Buddhist word for perfect peace and kindness. Buddhists believe that by following Buddha's teachings, a person can end their greed, hatred and **ignorance** (lack of knowledge). This breaks the circle of death and rebirth to end suffering. Then there is nirvana.

In our own words

"Nirvana, or Enlightenment, is a way of experiencing life. If, one day, I become free from greed, hatred and ignorance, I will see things just as they are. Then I won't expect things to last or to make me happy. This means I won't suffer when they don't!

As I am now, I may feel happy when I have cake in front of me, and a bit sad when it rains. But if I were Enlightened, my mood wouldn't depend on what was going on at the time. What a relief!"

Munisha, Member of the Western Buddhist Order, UK

◄ The eight-spoked Dhamma wheel is an important symbol in Buddhism. The spokes stand for the eight steps on the Noble Eightfold Path.

Theravada and Mahayana

Both Theravada and Mahayana Buddhists follow the Buddha's teachings. But Mahayana Buddhists follow later Buddhist teachers as well. They also worship heroic figures called **bodhisattvas** (see box below).

Bodhisattvas

In Mahayana Buddhism, a bodhisattva is a person who has gained Enlightenment and become a Buddha. Bodhisattvas put the happiness of others before their own. They delay reaching nirvana and choose to stay on earth to help others. People pray to them for help and guidance.

There are thousands of bodhisattvas. One of the most popular is Avalokiteshvara. He represents kindness and caring for others.

Avalokiteshvara is often shown with a thousand arms. This shows that he is ready to help everyone at once. He also has eleven heads and a thousand hands and eyes to help him see and help all suffering beings.

➤ *This Tibetan painting shows the bodhisattva, Avalokiteshvara. He is worshipped for his great pity and care for those who are suffering.*

Zen Buddhism

Zen Buddhism is a well-known type of Mahayana Buddhism. It is practised mainly in Japan and China. Buddhists use meditation as a way of finding the truth about life. But in Zen Buddhism, meditation is particularly important.

Zen Buddhists use different ways to help them meditate. These may be painting, writing poetry and gardening. They also use ancient forms of self-defence, such as karate.

Doing these things needs a lot of concentration and awareness. This helps them see life more clearly and behave more kindly.

Tibetan Buddhism

Buddhism became Tibet's main religion in the 14th century CE. Tibetan Buddhism includes lots of colourful ceremonies and many bodhisattvas are worshipped. Since 1959, China has controlled Tibet. This has put Tibetan Buddhism under threat (see page 43).

▼ *This Zen monk is dressed in his traditional black robes. Zen monks have to go through very strict training in meditation.*

Buddhism in daily life

All Buddhists try to follow the Buddha's example. They try to be kind, generous, truthful and patient. They believe that this will cause less suffering for themselves and others.

Buddhists believe that people are unkind because they don't know the truth about life. They think that having things will make them happy. Instead, it makes them selfish and greedy. People try to hold on to things, but Buddhism teaches that everything is always changing.

Buddhists believe that people need to be kinder, wiser and more contented with what they have got. Then they will move nearer to Enlightenment and happiness.

The Three Jewels

Buddhists put three things at the centre of their lives. They call them the Three Jewels. The first is the Buddha. The second is the Buddha's teachings (the Dhamma). The third is all Buddhists (the Sangha). Every day Buddhists recite these words:

'I go for refuge (safety) to the Buddha
I go for refuge to the Dhamma
I go for refuge to the Sangha.'

The Five Moral Precepts

Buddhists also make five promises, called the Five Moral Precepts. They promise:

1 Not to kill or harm living things

2 Not to steal

3 Not to behave badly or harmfully in a sexual way

4 Not to speak unkindly or tell lies

5 Not to drink alcohol or take drugs

▼ A monk meditates under a tree in Lumbini, the birthplace of the Buddha.

A Japanese Buddhist prays for peace in ➤ New York, USA. This is after the terrorist attacks of 11 September 2001.

In our own words

"I try to remember that everything I do, think and say has an effect on me and others. I meditate for about 45 minutes before breakfast. It helps me notice how I am feeling. If I know I'm in a bad mood, I can be careful not to take it out on others. I try to speak kindly, even when I disagree with someone.

I **recycle** as much of my rubbish as possible. This is to lessen my effect on our world. I love humour, and I have to work hard not to make hurtful jokes.

I can't be perfect, but I try my best, and apologize when I slip up."

Munisha, Member of the Western Buddhist Order, UK

Sacred texts

There are hundreds of sacred texts, or writings, in Buddhism. Some contain the Buddha's teachings. Others are writings by later Buddhist monks and teachers.

Chanting from the sacred texts is an important part of Buddhist practice. Chanting means reciting in a rhythmic way. Monks and nuns study the writings and help people to understand what they mean.

Collecting the texts

The Buddha's teachings were written down in the 1st century BCE. They were written in an ancient Indian language called **Pali**. These became the sacred texts of the Theravada Buddhists. Later texts were written in another ancient Indian language called **Sanskrit**.

▼ The Tipitaka *contains stories of the Buddha's past lives. This painting tells the story about Buddha appearing as an elephant to teach about generosity and gratitude in the story of the Goodness of the Elephant King.*

▲ *These pages are from a copy of the* Tipitaka. *The text is written in Pali on palm leaves. This is how the* Tipitaka *was first written down.*

The Tipitaka

The sacred texts of the Theravada Buddhists are called the **Tipitaka**. It is made up of three parts. The first part contains Buddha's rules for nuns and monks. The second contains Buddha's teachings. The third part of the *Tipitaka* is made up of writings that explain the Buddha's teachings.

---

weblinks

For more information about Buddhist sacred texts and some of the *Jataka* stories from the *Tipitaka*, go to www.waylinks.co.uk/series/religiontoday/Buddhism

---

The Metta Sutta

The Metta Sutta *is found in the second part of the* Tipitaka. *It is a famous talk given by the Buddha about the importance of* **metta**, *or loving kindness. Some Buddhists recite the Metta Sutta every day. Here is a part of it:*

'May all beings be well and happy, may their hearts be whole and pure! Whatever living beings there be – Weak or strong, tall or short, Small or large, seen or unseen, Living far or near, those who are Born and those yet to be born – May all beings, without exception, be happy!'

Mahayana Scriptures

Mahayana Buddhists have their own sacred texts. These are called '**sutras**'. Most of them were first written in Sanskrit from about the 1st century CE. Some are believed to be the actual word of the Buddha.

The Lotus Sutra

The *Lotus Sutra* is one of the most popular Mahayana texts. This sutra is a talk given by the Buddha to a huge gathering of followers. In it, he says that it is possible for everyone to gain Enlightenment.

The Diamond Sutra

The *Diamond Sutra* is part of a collection called the *Sutras of Perfect Wisdom*. Perfect Wisdom means gaining full knowledge about how things really are.

▼ *This is a page from the* Diamond Sutra, *one of the most important Mahayana sacred texts. It shows the Buddha teaching the monk Subhuti.*

▲ *In Tibet, sacred words called mantras are painted or carved on to prayer stones.*

The *Diamond Sutra* was written in about 300CE. Its main teaching is that nothing exists by itself. All things are connected. This is why nothing in the world is fixed.

Tibetan texts

The sacred texts of the Tibetan Buddhists are translations of Indian writings. They are divided into two sections called the *Kanjur* and the *Tenjur*. The *Kanjur* contains more than 1,000 texts of the Buddha's teachings. The *Tenjur* contains about 3,000 writings about the teachings.

Another famous Tibetan text is the *Bardo Thodrol*, or *Tibetan Book of the Dead*. When a person is dying, a monk reads to them from this book. The words are for guiding the person through the Bardo. This is a world between death and rebirth.

3 Practice, places of worship and holy days

Some Buddhists do not like to use the word 'worship' to describe how they show their beliefs. They feel this word suggests worship of God or a god. Many prefer the word 'practice' instead, or **puja**, an Indian word for ritual or prayer.

Buddhist practice can differ from country to country. But it usually includes honouring the Buddha at home or in the monastery or temple. Buddhists also mark festivals.

Visiting a temple

Buddhists may visit the temple at any time. At many temples, the monks lead puja (prayer) at set times of day.

A temple has a shrine room with images of the Buddha. Here Buddhists kneel and bow in front of the Buddha. They may bow three times, to the Buddha, the Dhamma (teachings) and the Sangha (monks and nuns). They may repeat the Three Jewels and also recite the Five Moral Precepts (see both on page 20).

Making offerings

As part of Buddhist practice, people may place flowers, candles and incense in front of the Buddha's image. Incense is perfumed sticks that are burned to give a sweet smell. Each offering has a special meaning:

- Fresh flowers will eventually droop and die. This reminds Buddhists that nothing lasts for ever.

- Candles light up a room. In the same way, the Buddha's teaching lights up people's lives.

- Like the Dhamma (the Buddha's teaching), the sweet smell of incense spreads everywhere. This reminds Buddhists about karma – that even their smallest actions have an effect.

weblinks

For more information about places of worship, go to www.waylinks.co.uk/series/religiontoday/Buddhism

▼ *These children are at a temple in London, UK. They show their respect for the Buddha by leaving offerings in front of his image.*

In our own words

"When we go to the temple we have to get up earlier than usual. We take some food to the monks for their midday meal and to share with our other friends. We wear white, because white is a symbol of purity.

We bow three times in respect to the Buddha and the monks. Then we chant in the ancient language of Pali. When the ceremony is nearly finished, we meditate for a few minutes.

Afterwards we help offer the midday meal for the monks. Then we sit together in a circle on the floor to share our lunch with the rest of the temple-goers."

Phra Nicholas Thanissaro, UK

Meditation

Meditation is central to Buddhist practice. Buddhists use it to train their minds. This way, they believe they can free themselves of ignorance, greed and hatred. It helps them to understand the truth about life. Through meditation, a person can calm the mind and experience peace.

Learning to meditate takes time. It also needs a good teacher. Many Buddhists meditate every day, either on their own or in a group.

There are many different kinds of meditation. Buddhists often sit in a quiet room with their eyes closed. They concentrate on their breathing.

Places of worship

Buddhist places of worship can be very different in style. The oldest places of Buddhist worship were the stupas. These were the dome-shaped mounds in northern India that contained the Buddha's ashes. Today, stupas are found all over the Buddhist world. Many contain holy

◄ *This white dome is the Swayambunath stupa in Kathmandu, Nepal. No one is sure exactly when it was built. The stupa has been an important Buddhist centre since the 1200s.*

▲ *A Buddhist pilgrim at the Jokhang Temple in Lhasa, Tibet. He is standing next to a row of giant prayer wheels. He spins these as he passes to release the prayers.*

objects or the remains of great Buddhist teachers. The design of the stupa is different in each country.

Places of pilgrimage

Many Buddhists like to make special journeys to stupas, shrines and places linked with the Buddha's life. For Tibetan Buddhists, the holiest site is the Johkhang Temple in Lhasa. It was built in 647 CE. Legend says the temple stands on the site of an underground lake in which people could see their future.

--- **weblinks** ---

For more information about the Jokhang Temple in Lhasa, Tibet, go to
www.waylinks.co.uk/series/religiontoday/Buddhism

Art and symbolism

Buddhist artists have created beautiful statues, paintings and carvings. But for hundreds of years after his death, they did not show the Buddha in person. Instead he was represented by symbols, such as footprints and the wheel that symbolizes his teachings. Buddha images first appeared in the 1st century CE.

Buddha images

Buddhists do not actually worship images of the Buddha. The images are to remind them of Enlightenment, of the Buddha's teachings and his special qualities.

Images show the signs that marked the Buddha as a very special human being. These include long earlobes and tightly curled hair. Mahayana Buddhists also have many images of bodhisattvas (see page 18).

➤ A modern image of the Buddha from a temple in Sri Lanka. It shows long earlobes and curled hair. His hands are in the teaching mudra.

Mudras

The hands and fingers of Buddha images are held in special ways. These are called **mudras**. In the fearlessness mudra, one hand is raised with its palm facing forward. In the meditation mudra, both hands rest in the lap. Another mudra has the Buddha touching the earth with one hand. This is what he did at his Enlightenment (see page 9). Both hands held together symbolizes teaching of the Dhamma.

Mandalas

*A **mandala** is a circular picture map showing the way to Enlightenment. It is used by Tibetan Buddhists to help them meditate.*

Around the outside of the mandala are three rings. The first is a ring of flames. This is to burn away unhelpful qualities such as greed, hatred and ignorance.

Inside the mandala are four open gateways leading to the centre. At each opening there is a picture of a bodhisattva. Each represents a quality such as wisdom or loving kindness.

As someone meditates on the mandala, his or her mind moves through the parts of the picture toward the centre. The centre means Enlightenment.

▼ *This mandala has been made from coloured sand by Tibetan monks. The mandala will later be destroyed at a special ceremony. This is a reminder of the Buddha's teaching that nothing lasts for ever.*

Buddhist festivals

There are many Buddhist festivals throughout the year. Some are linked to events from the Buddha's life. Others mark the lives of great Buddhist teachers or major events in Buddhist history.

Wesak

For Theravada Buddhists and many others, the most important festival is Wesak. It takes place in April or May to celebrate the Buddha's Enlightenment. Many people decorate homes and temples with lamps and candles. They may visit the temple for a special Wesak puja and to take gifts for the monks.

The sacred tooth

Another Theravada festival called Asala, or Dharma Day, takes place in July or August. This marks the first talk the Buddha made after his Enlightenment.

In Kandy, Sri Lanka, there are huge Asala parades. Decorated elephants move through the streets with dancers and musicians. One elephant has a golden casket on its back. It is a copy of the casket kept in the nearby Temple of the Tooth. It contains a tooth said to be one of the Buddha's.

▼ *This huge Wesak decoration comes from Sri Lanka. It shows the chariot in which Siddhattha rode when he saw the Four Sights (see page 8).*

Hana Matsuri

The festival of Hana Matsuri takes place in April. It is very important for Mahayana Buddhists in Japan. It marks the birth of the Buddha and is also a flower festival to celebrate the coming of spring.

Flower halls are set up in the temple grounds. These are reminders of the garden where the Buddha was born. Visitors pour scented tea over images of the baby Buddha.

▲ *Children in Japan dress up to celebrate the Hana Matsuri festival. They are wearing flowers in their hair to honour the Buddha.*

weblinks

For more information about a variety of Buddhist festivals, go to
www.waylinks.co.uk/series/religiontoday/Buddhism

In our own words

"On the day of Wesak, I usually take the day off work. I spend some time relaxing at home and the rest at the Buddhist Centre with my friends. At the Centre, some of us meditate together.

In the evening, loads of people meet at the Centre. We all bring food for a big shared meal and then go to the shrine hall. There's usually a talk about the the Buddha's Enlightenment and a special puja, or ritual. The puja celebrates his life and reminds us that we are trying to follow his example.

There is lots of chanting and readings. People light candles and incense in front of the Buddha figure.

Munisha, Member of the Western Buddhist Order, UK

4 Monks and monasteries

The Buddha spent a large part of his life living as a wandering holy man and teaching the Dhamma. Some Buddhists today leave their homes and belongings in the same way. They spend their lives learning and practising the Buddha's teachings. Together they form the Sangha, or community, of monks and nuns.

Becoming a monk

In many Theravada countries, young boys spend several months in a monastery as part of their education. Some then return to their families. Others stay to become monks.

The boys become monks in a special ceremony called **ordination**. In Sri Lanka, the ceremony dates back to the time of the Buddha. The young

▼ *These Sri Lankan boys are being ordained as monks. They are holding their new robes.*

monk has his head shaved. He asks a senior monk for permission to wear his monk's robes.

The Eight Requisites

Buddhist monks and nuns are only allowed to own eight items, known as the Eight Requisites. They have robes, a begging bowl, a belt and a water strainer for cleaning drinking water. They also have a walking stick, a toothpick, a needle and a razor (for monks). Everything else they use belongs to the monastery.

Western orders

The Friends of the Western Buddhist Order is one of the best-known Buddhist groups in Western countries (see page 44). The ordained people do not become monks or nuns.

Some teach and run Buddhist centres. Others have jobs that do good in some way. They may run Buddhist bookshops or vegetarian cafés. They may live in their own homes or with groups of Buddhists. Some have partners and children.

▼ *These women are being ordained as Buddhist nuns in Britain.*
They are at a monastery that follows Theravada Buddhism.

Rules for monks and nuns

Monks and nuns must follow strict rules. These rules were set down by the Buddha and are called the *vinaya*. Many monasteries have 227 rules, but the number can differ.

Rules include the Ten Moral Precepts. These are the Five Moral Precepts (see page 20) plus five other rules:

- Not eating after midday
- Not singing or dancing in fun
- Not wearing jewellery or perfume
- Not sleeping on a soft bed
- Not accepting goods or money

Life in the monastery

Monks and nuns live very simply. In Theravada monasteries, they rise early and eat only breakfast and lunch.

During the day the monks meditate and study the sacred texts. They lead ceremonies and puja for Buddhists who are not monks or nuns. Monks teach and guide anyone who wishes to learn about the Dhamma or asks for advice.

In a Zen monastery, life is very hard and strict. The monks meditate in the meditation hall. They also sleep on the floor there. They eat their simple meals in silence and spend long hours studying.

◄ *These monks are at the Jokhang Temple in Lhasa, Tibet. Reading from the sacred texts is a big part of their daily lives.*

▲ *These Zen monks are practising meditation in a Japanese monastery. They spend many hours each day learning to meditate.*

In our own words

"I am a nun in the Karma Kagyu tradition of Tibetan Buddhism. There were two reasons why I felt I wanted to take this commitment for the rest of my life. The first was an overwhelming (powerful) feeling that this was the only thing I wanted to do. Then I came to understand that becoming ordained (being made a nun) was the best way to make life meaningful and to become more useful to others.

That was over fifteen years ago and I have never regretted it. Life just gets better and better!"

Gelongma Konchok Lhamo, Kagyu Samye Ling Tibetan Centre, UK

weblinks

For more information about a Zen monastery, go to www.waylinks.co.uk/series/religiontoday/Buddhism

5 Buddhism and society

In Buddhist countries, such as Sri Lanka and Thailand, Buddhist monks and nuns play an important part in local life. Monasteries and temples are often used as schools and community centres. Ordinary people who are Buddhists support their local monastery. The monks teach people about the Dhamma and help them to live in a Buddhist way.

Right and wrong

Buddhists use the Five Moral Precepts (see page 20) and other teachings to guide them in life. But it is up to each person to make their own decisions about what is right and what is wrong.

Animal welfare

Buddhism teaches that people should avoid killing or harming living things. It also says they should become more loving and kind. To do this people should remember how it feels to suffer pain and fear. Then they will not wish to cause others pain.

The Buddha also taught that all actions have

◀ In Asia, elephants have been used for centuries to do work. Many are used to haul logs.

effects for the person doing them and for other living things. This has led some Buddhists to become involved in protecting the **environment**.

In Myanmar, Buddhists are working with others to protect elephants. The forests where the elephants live are being destroyed. Because of this, the elephants often move into farmland and damage crops. Sometimes elephants or people die as a result.

Buddhists are helping collect vital information about the elephants. They are also helping local people to live in peace with the elephants.

Vegetarianism

Many Buddhists choose not to eat meat because it means killing living things. But Buddhist teachings do not forbid people to eat meat. In some countries, meat is important if there is not much else to eat.

▼ *Monks receive gifts of food in Bangkok, Thailand. The monks take what is put in their begging bowls back to the monastery to eat.*

Engaged Buddhism

Many Buddhists are involved in what they call 'engaged Buddhism'. This means working to help people and the environment. Some work to set up hospitals and charities. Some are involved in politics and campaigning for peace. They do these things because Buddhism teaches them to have loving kindness for all living beings.

▼ *Palden Gyatsu is a Tibetan monk who was imprisoned for many years by the Chinese. Here he leads a protest against Britain selling weapons to other countries.*

International network

The International Network of Engaged Buddhists (INEB) began in Thailand in 1989. It now has members in 33 countries. It combines Buddhist practice with taking action to make the world a more just and peaceful place. People who are not Buddhists can join the INEB. They must want to help others because

---

weblinks

For information about another example of 'engaged Buddhism', go to www.waylinks.co.uk/series/religiontoday/Buddhism

---

they feel sorrow for their suffering. One of the main jobs for the INEB is to help people affected by war. They try to help these people solve their problems without using violence.

Drug rehabilitation

Another example of 'engaged Buddhism' is the work of the Wat Tham Krabok. This is a monastery in Thailand that helps addicts to give up drugs and alcohol. The treatment is strict, but very successful.

Prison visiting

The Angulimala Buddhist Prison Chaplaincy Organisation was set up in Britain in 1985. It was named after a murderer and robber named Angulimala who became a follower of the Buddha. A team of Buddhists visit prisons to teach prisoners about Buddhism. The prisoners do not have to be Buddhists to be taught.

▼ Drug addicts take part in a Buddhist ceremony in the Wat Tham Krabok monastery in Thailand.

6 Buddhism in the 21st century

For many Buddhist countries, the 20th century was a difficult time. In countries such as China, Tibet and Myanmar, Buddhists were badly treated and even killed for their beliefs. This situation has continued into the 21st century.

All over the world, people are getting more interested in wealth and less interested in a simple life. The Buddha taught that greed causes suffering. Despite this, Buddhism is becoming popular again in places such as India. It is also spreading to new places in Europe, Australia and North America.

weblinks
For more information about Tibet and the Tibetan Government-in-Exile, go to www.waylinks.co.uk/series/religiontoday/Buddhism

◄ The Dalai Lama is the leader of Tibet's Buddhists. He now lives in Dharamsala, India.

The Dalai Lama

The Dalai Lama is Tibet's religious leader and was its ruler. In 1959 the Chinese government took control of Tibet. It did not want people to practise religion of any kind. Hundreds of Buddhist monasteries were destroyed. Thousands of monks were imprisoned or killed.

The Dalai Lama now lives in India. He is famous for his warmth, wisdom and feeling for others. He travels all over the world trying to win support for the Tibetan people and suggesting peaceful ways to solve their problems.

Buddhism in India

By the 12th century CE, Buddhism had almost disappeared from India. Now Buddhism is again becoming popular there. One of the reasons for this is the work of Dr B.R. Ambedkar.

Ambedkar was a **Hindu** who fought for equality in Hindu society. He became a Buddhist just before his death in 1956. Millions of Hindus followed him. Ambedkarite Buddhists are India's largest Buddhist group

▼ *Dr Ambedkar speaks to a large crowd in India in 1956. At this event, thousands of Hindus became Buddhists.*

Buddhism in the West

Buddhism reached the West at the end of the 19th century CE. This happened when Buddhist texts were translated. At the same time, people from Buddhist countries in Asia began to settle in Europe and North America. Later, Westerners became interested in Buddhism.

Friends of the Western Buddhist Order

The Friends of the Western Buddhist Order (see page 35) was started by an English Buddhist monk, the Venerable Sangharakshita. This movement combines different types of Buddhism and is suited to Western society. For example, members do not wear robes and do not become monks or nuns. The order is based in the United Kingdom.

New Buddhist movements

The Soka Gakkai is one of the fastest-growing Buddhist groups in the West. It was formed in 1930 and was based on the teachings of a Japanese monk. It teaches chanting as a way to bring good health, happiness and wealth. It set up centres in the USA in the 1960s and in Europe in the 1970s and 1980s.

▼ *A member of the Western Buddhist Order at a temple in Manchester, UK. Members wear scarves around their necks for special ceremonies.*

weblinks
For more information about the Friends of the Western Buddhist Order, go to www.waylinks.co.uk/series/religiontoday/Buddhism

In our own words

The future of Western Buddhism

"I think Buddhism will continue growing in the West. Buddhism emphasizes loving kindness. It says that each of us can change our own lives and the world. We can do this by taking responsibility for the results of our actions.

People will find that greed is causing more and more damage to society and the environment. Many may begin to see Buddhism as an attractive and effective way forward.

In Western Buddhism we will continue to see three particular changes taking place:

1 *Women will be taken much more seriously than they have been.*

2 *Western Buddhists who are not monks may study, meditate and teach as much as monks or nuns.*

3 *Western Buddhists will become more involved in politics and in working to help people."*

Munisha, Member of the Western Buddhist Order, UK

▼ *A Buddhist temple in Los Angeles, USA. In the 21st century, Buddhism may become more popular in countries outside its Asian homeland.*

weblinks

For more information about modern Buddhism, go to www.waylinks.co.uk/series/religiontoday/Buddhism

Glossary

arahant (Sanskrit: *arhat*) The Pali word for an Enlightened person whose mind is free from hatred, ignorance and greed.

Bodhi Tree The tree under which the Buddha is believed to have gained Enlightenment.

bodhisattva An heroic figure in Mahayana Buddhism who has gained Enlightenment and become a Buddha. Out of pity and love for the world, the bodhisattva chooses to help other people end their suffering.

caste The classes or divisions in Hindu society.

chanting Reciting in a rhythmic way.

Dhamma (Sanskrit: *Dharma*) The Pali word for the Buddha's teaching.

Enlightenment The experience of understanding the truth about the world and how things really are.

environment The natural world or the conditions around us.

Hindu A follower of Hinduism. Hinduism is a religion that involves many gods and goddesses. It is the main religion of India.

ignorance Lack of knowledge.

karma (Pali: *kamma*) The Sanskrit word for the good and bad actions that affect people's future happiness in this and other lives.

Mahayana One of the two main schools of Buddhism. It means 'the great way'.

mandala A circular picture that Tibetan Buddhists use to help them meditate. In their minds, they follow a path into the centre of the picture, like following a map.

meditation A central part of Buddhist practice, the aim of meditation is to quiet or still the mind in order to develop peace and awareness.

metta (Sanskrit: *maitri*) The Pali word for loving kindness without expecting anything in return.

mudra (Pali: *mudda*) The Sanskrit word for the position of the hands in images of the Buddha and bodhisattvas.

nirvana (Pali: *nibbana*) The perfect peace and happiness entered when the cycle of birth and rebirth is broken and suffering ends.

ordination A ceremony of commitment. In Buddhism, this usually means becoming a monk or nun.

Pali An ancient Indian language in which the texts of the Theravada Buddhists were first written down.

parinirvana (Pali: *parinibbana*) The Sanskrit word for the Buddha's death.

puja The name given to a ceremony of devotion and worship in Buddhism and Hinduism.

recycle Break down waste materials so they can be reused.

sacred Holy.

Sangha The community of Buddhists. For some Buddhists, the Sangha particularly means monks and nuns. For others, it includes all Buddhists.

Sanskrit An ancient Indian language in which many Mahayana sacred texts are written down.

stupa A dome-shaped Buddhist monument.

sutra (Pali: *sutta*) The Sanskrit word for a short Buddhist sacred text.

Theravada One of the two main schools of Buddhism. It means 'way of the elders'.

Tipitaka (Sanskrit: *Tripitaka*) The Pali word for the sacred texts of the Theravada Buddhists.

vinaya The rules for Buddhist monks and nuns.

Zen A school of Mahayana Buddhism from China and Japan. The word Zen means 'meditation'.

Timeline

c.623 BCE	Siddhattha Gotama born in Lumbini, Nepal
c.588 BCE	Siddhattha gains Enlightenment in Bodh Gaya, India, and becomes the Buddha
c.543 BCE	The Buddha passes away in Kushinagar, India
c.543-443 BCE	Buddhism splits into the Theravada and Mahayana schools
268-239 BCE	Reign of Emperor Ashoka Maurya in India. Buddhism becomes the major faith of India.
c.250 BCE	Buddhism reaches Sri Lanka and later, Myanmar
1st century BCE	*Tipitaka* is written down
1st century CE	Buddhism reaches China. First images of the Buddha made.
4th century CE	Buddhism reaches Korea
7th century CE	Buddhism reaches Tibet
6th century CE	Buddhism reaches Japan
12th century CE	Buddhism almost disappears from India. Zen Buddhism reaches Japan from China.
13th century CE	Buddhism the official religion in Thailand, Cambodia and Laos
1907	First Buddhist Society in Britain formed
1930	Buddhist Society of America formed
1935	The present Dalai Lama born in Tibet
1956	In India, Dr Ambedkar converts many people to Buddhism
1967	Friends of the Western Buddhist Order founded in the UK
1989	International Network of Engaged Buddhists begins in Thailand

Further reading

Buddhist Prayer and Worship by Anita Ganeri (Franklin Watts, 2006)

Celebrations: Wesak by Anita Ganeri (Heinemann Library, 2002)

DK Eyewitness Guides: Buddhism by Philip Wilkinson (Dorling Kindersley, 2003)

The Facts About Buddhism by Alison Cooper (Hodder Wayland, 2007)

Great Names: Buddha by Anna Carew-Miller (Mason Crest Publishers, 2002)

World Beliefs and Cultures: Buddhism by Sue Penney (Heinemann, 2003)

Index